VERSE INFERNAL

Poetry Inspired by the Satanic Religion

Aperient Press

Edited by Ronald J. Murray & Ruth Waytz

Edited by RJ Murray and Ruth Waytz

Interior design by Arun Lakshmanan
Cover design by V Holecek

Publisher's gratitude to the Maestro and the Muse.

APERIENT PRESS
50-855 Washington St. Suite 2C #323
La Quinta CA 92253
info@aperientpress.com
www.aperientpress.com

APERIENT PRESS

DEDICATION

For Anton Szandor LaVey and the Church of Satan

Contents

"Glory and praise to you, O Satan, in the heights
Of Heaven where you reigned and in the depths
Of Hell where vanquished you dream in silence!
Grant that my soul may someday repose near to you
Under the Tree of Knowledge, when, over your brow,
Its branches will spread like a new Temple!"

— Charles Baudelaire, *Les Litanies de Satan*
(William Aggeler translation, 1954)

ACKNOWLEDGEMENTS

The Editors would like to thank the following for their support throughout the creation of this work:

Peter H. Gilmore and Peggy Nadramia for upholding this philosophy, which has been so important for those around the globe who have found their reflection in it, and for continuing the organization which represents it so fiercely and responsibly.

Hydra M. Star for her excitement, support, and for sharing her publishing expertise.

Sara Tantlinger, Stephanie M. Wytovich, and Nicholas Day for their support and mentorship in poetry over the years, through which I have built the expertise needed to curate this collection.

Most importantly, the poets who have made this collection a possibility through their hard work.

INTRODUCTION

Satan has always been a friend to the poet. His influence on the genre has a long reach into the depths of human history. His mythical lair has been fantasized about and explored by Dante Alighieri in his *Divine Comedy*. His fall from Heaven and subsequent rise as the Ruler of Hell was romanticized by John Milton in *Paradise Lost*. And he found his sympathy with Charles Baudelaire's *Le Fleurs du mal*.

For the first time in history, Satan's religion, as founded by Anton Szandor LaVey in 1966, and further defined in 1969 with the publication of *The Satanic Bible*, is expressed through a collection of poetry written by His Infernal Legion: members of the Church of Satan.

On the pages between these covers, Satan's mighty principles blaze with the hot Hellfire of passionate verse. You'll find a flourishing lust for life, the proud and prodding trident of vengeance, the relentless pursuit of gratification in all the so-called sins, the magic of comedy, and the ominous drumbeat found in wild celebration of our unholy Holidays.

I beam with Satanic pride in doing the Devil's work, putting these poems into the world which he rules with fervor and pleasure.

    — Ronald J. Murray
      May 31, LVII A.S.

GRIGORI T. CROSS

Born to a mother with a degree in English literature, Grigori T. Cross developed a taste for the written word early in life and wrote his first poem before he reached the age of 10. College brought accolades from his English and philosophy professors, who noted his usage of romantic phrasing in essays and encouraged him to develop his talent. Studying philosophy at UC Berkeley introduced him to subtle ways he could use language to bring the details in his stories to life. With a newfound appreciation for the written word, he authored an erotic novella (*The Satyr of New Orleans*), a handful of short stories (to be found in *The Ladies and Gentlemen of Horror* 2017 and the December 2021 issue of *The Crow's Quill*), and even a poem, "Hell," published in the *San Diego Union-Tribune*. Nowadays, when he's not writing fiction or essays or composing music, Mr. Cross writes answers to absurd questions at grigoritcross.com from the comfort of his home in southern California.

LITTLE SONG, LITTLE HORN

When lions eat their conquered prey, it's right!
Behold the glory o' nature's power i' full!
So Satan meets your dogma with his might
and immolates the stifling doctrines null!

What next? He takes some time alone to think
and conjures carnal, living thoughts to speak.
The Devil's pen is filled to brim with ink,
and drips with wisdom real occultists seek.

Magicians learn their glam'rous tricks from him—
an undertaking not for th' faint of heart.
The energy turns th' brightest light bulbs dim;
fear not: great Belial has done his part.

…and tidal waves, as night turns into day;
Leviathan must also have his say.

These tasty words were written by a man
whose insight's now recorded, teeth all bared,
for us. Rejoice! No holy writ can fan
our flames to heights where Heav'n itself is scared!

Like mirrors are these pages 'fore me now,
so much that I'd have written them myself.
I've read them. I'm awakening my vow
to cultivate and love my sense of self!

Whatever glory's here within my reach
is mine to take without reserve, with glee.
Now I deliver unto you a speech
that will endear, enamor you of me.

The world's an oyster. I'm to find my pearl.
Relax and watch my sorcery unfurl.

OF TWELVE, OF THREE, OF SIX, OF NINE O'CLOCK

High noon's got shoulders wide, some narrow hips,
a pioneer's perspective, fire 'neath
his feet. And, oh! He doesn't like to chew.
He's selfish, solar, worthy—human, too.
He wants attention always. Boredom's not
becoming; glamor's favored. Power's up
for grabs and he will take it where he can.
Insisting 'pon himself is not his most
endearing trait, but patience pays so well.

The witching hour's best described as svelte,
and towers over his inferiors.
A social critic, misanthropic, he's
the studied kind with sagely intellect,
his mind a guide to undefiled truth.
Professors seek his counsel all the time.
If lost in thought you find him, don't be shocked.
He revels in his theories. I'm afraid
his revolutions, revelations sing
the same tritonic chord. Beware, beware.

The evening is distinctly feminine.
She graces us with generosity
and offers her devotion free to those
deserving few. Her legs go on for days.
She dances like a fallen angel, ha!
A nurturer at heart, she elevates
and conjures all the best she sees within
us. Balanced poise her greatest strength and woe,

she bears the weight of Atlas, smiling full.
She's soft in body only—heed thee well.

The Devil's hour! Oh, how under-loved!
His ways to win are many; he will find
them all. A walking belly laugh, ho ho!

He's up for any scheme and company,
his actions speaking louder than his words.
Gregarious, built like a tree—a great
redwood, most probably—he watches quite
observantly o'er all he loves that he
can see. He's built as thick as lumber, round
all 'round. Go watch him beat the tympani!

The corners of the clock are thus described.
This knowledge bids you leave th' "occult" behind.

IX

Hark: you wake the Dragon!

Here is wisdom: life is drenched
and drips with blood,
so rip and rend, move just so
those brittle sinews which move
'gainst the Dragon should break—
so thirst may be quenched
by life's bittersweet elixir.
Nine-fold I affirm you,
Great Accuser, King Womb!
Witness: I sweep the Darkness
with my profane Left Hand
and am regaled with carnal tongue
by th' bounty of vi'lent Earth,
birthing formed and dancing stars.
Storm-born, I am virile
and succor impious delights

The "madman" heralds me,
and yea, ye shall see his prophecy
unfold in your sight.
Ah, you give the sign of an open eye!
Make way,
for I am the laughing mouth dancing in fire.
I am the gaping mouth of dirt and will.
Lo, the adamantine gates swing open,
and from yawning jaws the lightning spills
to forge the id
to forge ego

O, waking life! The Is-To-Be!

Hail, Ownmost, true Father Time!
From the abyss, I call forth
My serpentine conscience!
The Black Flame calls my Lord – WOLLEN!
Tone and pitch direct my Lord – DRACARYS!
Holiness stunned the beast, bade me worship the sun
and would pervert my affections 'til 'way from it mine eyes
could not turn
But the void does not lie. Though my attentions may be diverted,
what takes my eyes must take my body must consume me whole,
and to swallow me thus is to release the viral flood of life into blinding
death!

Solar light is blinding, yet hailed as a hero.
Lunar light's the mirror, reflecting one, not zero.
I am no longer melting in the sun.
Sum lux ex tenebris, zero become one.
As summoned, so invoked,
Alive and fire-soaked;
I met my shadow in ethereal catacombs
And gave myself authenticity—

TOTAL DEMONIC SUPREMACY!

Pure, primordial pollutants pulse in pairs opposed;
'twas vicious vital instinct broke the dam—
brilliance bolstered by base blasphemy.
Ah, but I beg the question,
for primal fire's damper burned
Is but atavistic return.

Hear me:

When my words slither from your lips in a spiral of smoke
When I step out from the crackle and dancing shadows to meet you
My name will be formed from the ashes of volcanoes reborn:
The beast and the *logos*—the pure, imperfect host.
The Greeks knew my name among the Titans
I am the harbinger of immaterial tragedy:
wisdom for few, destruction for all,
death, pestilence, the sweetest carnal revelries,
laughter in the face of raining bloodshed,
turgid, sopping lust in the struggle for power,
ALL of this and more is the price of intoxication.
Lapping at the fountainhead of the elixir of life—
These are the rewards of the Son of Time

Darkness drapes a cursed veil over your eyes,
th' lone symbol best exemplifying the sick paradox:
eternity is the price of liberty
and signifies its own justification.
Through wizened illusion, gnashing teeth shine
through to the waking life of the burning star in your eye,
and here am I, become as the black hole at the bottom of life,

with support from the pit, verily the magician's wish,
uttering opposition and proposition, the fertile soil of contradiction.

C'est la vie!

All three of my pieces were inspired directly by Satanic literature. *Of Twelve, of Three, of Six, of Nine O'Clock* is a soliloquy-ode to the LaVey Synthesizer Clock featured in *The Satanic Witch*. *Little Song, Little Horn* is two sonnets in one poem; the first half takes its inspiration from the books in *The Satanic Bible*, whereas the second half is a poetic rendering of the reaction Satanists have while reading it for the first time. *IX* was conceived of as a lyric poem, but has found its home as a prose poem, at once a vessel by which I might introduce a phrase or two into the greater Satanic conversation and a bombastic burst of spirit, drawing inspiration from all the Satanic thought I had absorbed up to the point of its writing. Each piece was a labor of love, an act of creation indulged in as only Satanists can.

DAVID INGRAM

David Ingram is the lead vocalist for the legendary death metal band Benediction, and he is involved in many other musical projects. He is a Reverend in the Church of Satan and has been a member for 14 years. He loves his dogs and enjoys drinking a beer or 12. He is absolutely bonkers about the British television show Doctor Who.

"Remember: there's no point in being grown-up if you can't be childish sometimes."

ARE YOU AFRAID?

Covert comrades in darkness dwell
No faith in a Heaven or Hell
Indulgence is now crystal clear
He did create a religion feared

Philosophy for the elite
Statements nine, substratum seat
Eleven rules upon the Earth
As a Satanist from birth

A proud rebel, a blackened lair
Show respect or do not go there
Study, not worship, Lex Satanicus
Carnal nature overrides
Self-sacrificial sons

Codified philosophy
The Left Hand Path was laid
His work intrinsic
Are you afraid?

WISDOM UNDEFILED

Wisdom undefiled, a force to fill the void
Knowledge resonating power,
Its acumen to reign unsoiled
Hollow empty postures
The elite to ascertain
Such archaic pious monsters
Let wisdom undefiled remain

Through undefiled wisdom
The illogical is scorned
We're intellectually developed
Satanists born

Aghast foresight, burned in pride
A sin to revel in, never hide
Sacerdotal Christian pales
Before undefiled wisdom

THE LEVIATHAN

Prodigious adornment invokes the goat gargantuan
symbol of the sinister, Leviathan

Resonance of parallel ornamentation
Symbolized our illumination
Iconoclasts those rebellious ones to cross the Styx
Codified: Satanism, 1966

They feed their pious nightmares
A philosophy so feared
Black flames to guard the Sigil
Our symbol is revered

Embraced by our Cabal
This Leviathan illuminates
Proudly throwing open wide
The Adamantine gates

The pieces I submitted here are all adapted from lyrics I have written for my project band Echelon, the albums *The Brimstone Aggrandizement* (2017) and the forthcoming *Open Wide The Adamantine Gates*. The inspiration for the latter album title was from Magus Gilmore's introduction to *The Satanic Bible*. The phrase had such power that I had to incorporate it into the album title. Said submissions are *Are You Afraid?*, *Undefiled Wisdom*, and *The Leviathan*. All should be somewhat familiar to the discerning Satanist.

DRACONIS BLACKTHORNE

Rev. Blackthorne is author of several books on the subject of Satanism, the occult, philosophy, misanthropy, parapsychology, Lesser & Greater Magic, Art & Poetry. He is also the Editor-In-Chief of *The Devil's Diary* magazine, as well as various "Black Arts & Witch Crafts" multimedia projects. Works have appeared in publications including *The Black Flame*, *The Cloven Hoof*, *The Trident*, and *Not Like Most*. Interviews can be found on Radio Free Satan and a ritual sequence with Magistra Blanche Barton on Pact with The Devil presentation. Interests include Horror, Criminology, Abnormal Psychology, Parapsychology, Metaphysics, Weight Training, Martial Arts, Erotica, & Dark History.

WALPURGIS HEXENNACHT

Black Moon and Eclipse
Opens the Portals of Hell
Deepest darkness of The Abyss
Flickering shadows in the mist
Malefic Music of The Night
Madly dancing carnal delights
Beauty burning in Lust
Supping The Devil's Cauldron of Might
Potions immortal, strigas take flight
Pentagram glows with third Evil Eye
666, The Triune sight
Hexennacht, Hell's Bells resound
Echoes of Unhallowsnacht
Gently calls from beyond
Infernal Throne, Hellflames emerge
Arising western cragged mountain summit
Hades upon horizon dusk
Encircled with demons and imps and witches
Phantom procession, sinister path
Basilisk slither and glide, upon the Nocturne tide
Grimoires of Power, Words come to Be
Dimensions of space and time-lessness
'Sacrificial' Bonefires alight! Fumigation Sorcery
Drægon emerge, the angles, The Gates
Waxen torches lead the way to and from The Underworld
Red eyes in the darkness, hooves quake the earth
Wicked Wings, Winds return...

VERNAL EQUINOX LVII

Season Leviathan stirs as the wyrmoon shines bright in the western sky
Lightning bolt through pentagonal portal thrown
Igniting Hellfire upon the horizon wherein we are drawn
Descending into the waters of Styx, Cocytus, Zamzam, Phlegethon
Arise to greet the stars, mighty behemoths of the deep!
Ouroboros encircles the earth in Hellemental alternation
The Garden of Dark Delights beckons in verdant invigoration, unholy sinful exhilaration
Calling forth devil satyrs and daemonic nymphs to dance in fertile fields of carnal lust!
Imbibing the nectars of pleasure and partaking ambrosia sublime!

DUSKENING CALLS

When the sun sinks into Hell
You can see the pit flames there
Upon the horizon for all to see

Creatures of Hellemental fane
Come to fly, swim, and creep
Caverns of Belial's domain deep

The Duskening calls
Children of Satan all
Draegon wings, western demon winds
Coursing across the land and sea

Lucifer's star
Glitters by Hecate's moonlight
Reflecting Sorath's Might
Constellations reveal occult mysteries

The Duskening calls
To those born of darkness

Mark of The Beast, blackest heart
Debauchery and Sorcery

Nocturnal Orchestra
Floats along the evening gusts
By the zephyrs and the trees
From ancient tales of sithening

As Satan's cloak envelopes the land
The western pentagram is cast
And daemons of every shape and size
Come forth to partake in wicked delights

Walpurgis Hexennacht: A celebration of one of our Highest UnHolidays. *Vernal Equinox LVII*: In verdant appreciation for burgeoning flora and fauna, and the fertile energies pervasive. *Duskening Calls*: Those Magical moments when the sun lapses into the horizon, likened descending into Hell, which is environmentally detectible in coloration.

RICK POWELL

Rick Powell lives in Oak Forest, Illinois. He is a lover of horror and dark fiction and his poetry and stories have appeared in numerous publications including *Infernal Ink Magazine*, and most recently, *Lustcraftian Horrors: Erotic stories inspired by H.P. Lovecraft*. His poetry books are titled *My Soul Stained My Seed Sour* and *More Regrets Than Glories*. Goodreads: https://www.goodreads.com/author/show/8442207.Rick_Powell   Facebook: https://www.facebook.com/tenebraerick Twitter: @tenebraerick

A TOAST

May you reign in obscurity and your false idols flourish,
Your hopes become naught and your faith leave your side,
May your trials bear down on you like a leaf in the sand,
Tribulations awash over you and carry you in their tide.

May the false deeds you do tarnish the mask that you wear,
The puppetry you exhibit will be your one and only dance,
May the hypocrisy that you breed be your only spoiled child,
The seed that your loins spew be your grasping last chance.

My wish is for you to wallow in your own brand of insecurity,
To forever have doubt in your heart, to have apathy in your will,
My wish is for you to always disappoint the ones in your circle,
To reap a constant earth of mistrust in all the fields that you instill.

My wish is your agony so sweet as I raise this glass of fine wine,
Crimson like my hatred for you, cold as the ice of your very soul,
My wish, as I take a sip and then toss this glass into the hearth fire,
Is to laugh at your helplessness, for over me, you have no control.

HATPIN

I hold it in my hand, the needle glints so sleek,
The head of this pin is a jewel of the brightest jade,
I know not the craftsman who created such a fine item,
It feels like part of my soul, for my grip it was specifically made.

I used it one time, on a gentleman who once accosted me,
His body was a rank of odor, his breath smelling of drink,
He tore at my finest blouse, clawed at my exposed breast,
I pulled the pin from my bonnet, in his groin it did sink.

He shrieked and gasped for air, as he fell on the cobblestone,
I was shaking and shivering, knowing not what came over me,
As he was moaning, his body prostrate on the lamp lit street,
I continued to stab him again, not caring that someone would see.

My vision became crimson, the devil had invaded my spirit,
I lost the number of times that I pierced his bloated, vile form,
As I straightened up panting, wearing a smile of satisfaction,
I felt his blood dripping down my face in a torrent ever so warm.

Not a soul had known what I had done, a secret I will never share,
I wear that pin in my bonnet proudly as I walk down the crowded
street,
My heart is eager for the next time, the next wretch to bring me
misfortune,
I yearn for that evil devil to return, to consume my heart with its fiery
heat.

THE MIDNIGHT HOUR

It is the time when the mortal forms succumb to rest,
The time to put your troubles and toils away till the morrow,
To not think about what has ailed you or hampered your mind,
To try to forget who has harmed you or has caused you to sorrow.

This hour is for other things to come to life and rise from the shadows,
Things the light of day had not exposed and revealed to human eyes,
Things that have no home here in the waking dawn of daily man,
This hour is for creatures of many forms to stalk under the ebony
skies.

Some have claw or talon that can rip asunder your flesh in a minute,
Teeth that are razor sharp that will stop your scream before it has
spoken,
Some are the most savage beasts of nightmares that you brain could
ever conceive,
That to gaze upon them for a moment will leave your frail mind and
soul broken.

Foolish is the man who would brave to venture out into this hellish
world,
To try to show wisdom and courage and prove they are not the ones to
cower,
Beware of these beings that are known to haunt the darkest of all
graves,
It is far better to stay in your homes and not seek what walks at the
midnight hour.

Hatpin was inspired by Satanic Rules #4, 5, & 11. The rules that all Satanists should live by. *A Toast* was inspired by The Ritual of Destruction. A personal one, you might say. It was a ritual in itself when I wrote this, and the outcome when I completed it had the results I expected. *The Midnight Hour* was inspired by Halloween (of course). Nothing brings about the awe and wonder of childhood like that spooky night of ghosts and goblins.

ROBERT J. LEUTHOLD

Robert J. Leuthold was born on November 3, 1977, a few months ahead of schedule and with cerebral palsy. As if to set a precedent, his birth was far from normal. After defying medical odds and living through the night despite being a traumatic, premature birth, he also became one of the first mainstreamed children in his area. His childhood was as normal as someone in his unique physical situation could expect. Though she denies it, Robert's mother influenced his passion for horror and the darker side of life via exposure to Stephen King and classic horror movies, which remain a staple in his creative diet to this day, along with various extreme genres of music. His first long-term writing stint was for Hydra M. Star's *Infernal Ink Magazine*, which in turn led to being featured in *The Ladies and Gentlemen of Horror*, curated by Jennifer L. Miller, for the years 2015 and 2016. He is the author of *Obsidian Odes: A Collection of Erotic Horror Verse* from Infernal Ink Books. Robert currently resides in Louisiana. When he isn't writing twisted poetry or drinking copious amounts of coffee, he can be found on Facebook: www.facebook.com/RobertJLeuthold

THE DEVIL'S FANE

The congregation gathers
on this most profane evening
for unholy rites.
Baphomet's sigil 'pon Western wall
over the proceedings
The Cornu, raised
Infernal Names and desires spoken
We have taken thy names
as a part of ourselves
Wielding the unholy Powers,
both ritual and mundane,
To manifest our Wills
upon the world
Of, but separate from it.
As beasts we are,
As beasts we remain,
Proudly numbered among
The Devil's Fane.

LIFE

What is life?
The sum of all experience,
An overflowing chalice.
Drink deeply,
Live proudly,
Lust and love unashamedly,
Hate as well.
Clutch life by the throat,
As one should,
For it is all we have.
Ride it into submission.
Make it yours.
Life everlasting,
World without End!
Joy to the Flesh,
Forever!

THE HELLFIRE RISES (A RITUAL CHARGE)

I feel the all too familiar warmth in my gut—
The time has come again.
On this Walpurgis eve, the earth trembles
Upon the Brocken, devils gather.

As one, we raise our hands,
and give the sign of the Horns.
Hell's Adamantine gates swing wide,
and as I call the names,
my desires are made manifest.

Asmodeus the destroyer,
flanked by Mother Kali,
rides forth upon Hell's hot winds,
poised to reap a grim destruction
upon those who have betrayed or opposed me.

On this night, the Hellfire rises,
consuming all that was
to usher in a new life:

Cleansing.
Hope.

It burns away
Old and useless scars,
immolating that which
is no longer needed.

I open my mouth
in a wordless scream,
and time stops.
The air pulses momentarily,
as lightning splits the sky in twain,
Almost as a sign
from Satan himself.

I take a ragged, rasping breath,
And the ritual continues.
More desires are thrown
upon Hell's hot Winds,
And still, the Hellfire rises.

My poetry was inspired by the second and seventh Satanic Statements in particular. I have a lust for life, and all without being worth a million in prizes (more like tree fiddy ;). I digress, and on a serious note…. My hardwired survival instinct, my ability to adapt and thrive despite the odds runs through my poetry, as well as nods to Ritual magic. As this little primer before (or after, depending on placement, edit as needed) shows, I embody the needed sense of humor to work my mojo baby, yeah! The poetry I'd written, and, in some cases, rediscovered, was inspired by my life, the most Satanic thing of all.

A.S.C.

A.S.C. lives in an apartment overlooking a big city somewhere in North America. Her view of the ebb and flow of life underneath her window often provides her with living examples of the Satanic principles in motion.

INSCRIBED

An inscription on a page
From between the covers
Of a book I bought
From a vending machine
Taught me more about life
Than living has so far

Looking at my hand
reading the lines
Mercury Venus Mars and Moon
What do they say
Besides Knapp's Root Beer
Purifies the blood
As luck would have it

Picking out a card
Major minor mentor
The Hierophant wears a triple crown
And the keys to everything
Are at his feet
But still, he can't decide what kind
Of advice to give

The light it wins
When it tricks us into thinking
That we can't see without it
But you believe in things
you can't see all the time
And hope throws stars into the sky
For wishing on

Making me wonder
If you ever knew
Anything at all
Or if you've just been
Guessing, inscribed with half-truths
Making choices from
Books and lines and cards
And stars.

THEATRICS

The air is charged, electric, static, it shocks my lungs with each inhale.
I'm waiting for the curtain to rise, watching the golden rope
in the stage man's hands.
They twitch, those hands, they tense, like a magician's
as he waits to release the rabbit.
I may divide in half, inside my own box, just standing here.

The red velvet pulsates in the lights,
does it rise or does it writhe?
It waits to reveal what has been built behind damask,
deep breaths drawing fabric to ribs, starved free of fat. In and out,
bellows from the belly of
that which waits behind.
I wait and watch, the rabbit inside the hat,
shallow breathed and ready.
The first chord rings, resounding distraction from my focused gaze.
I miss the slight of hand, that which is bound, released

by opened fingers. Brocade sways,
wayside,   revealing all.

There they stand, maestros, minstrels, magic men.

I am whole, charmed by prestidigitation, unloosed again.

6 O'CLOCK

I watched the sun
Dance along the wire
And wondered what it was sending
Along with the 6 o'clock news

A collection of imps
Swaying in reds and golds
Sending mixed messages
Nixing the negatives
on a tightrope

Old story, yesterday's news
Light versus dark
old world gods
Fighting inconsequential wars
With forgotten means

Like tinsel on the highway
Weaving between cars
Decorating the in between
Joy in an ugly scene
Like us

Dancing on the wire,
Strange flames flicking
In blackened spaces
Along with the 6 o'clock news

Inscribed was inspired by the 2nd Satanic Statement, where the author was busy living and enjoying things that brought her pleasure (like buying random books in a vending machine), at a local carnival and noticed the tight-eyed, desperate people in line waiting to have their fortunes read. The contrast of living a vital existence over clinging to spiritual pipedreams added a particular flair to the day. *Theatrics* is an ode to the 7th Satanic Rule of the Earth; it's an acknowledgement of the power of a realized moment after a particularly intense working. Given A.S.C.'s interest in live performances of all kinds, it's not hard to picture her at this moment. *6 o'clock* is an homage to the 5th Satanic sin. A.S.C.'s has spent the past few years observing the propagation of herd mentality in those who think they are above it all. While watching the sun set, one of her favorite pastimes, she was struck by the idea of all the homes below her receiving an influx of their latest fix. There may be a little side dish of awareness of self-deceit served with this one too.

DAX BORDAS

I have been a member of the Church of Satan for 16 years and an active member for just over a decade now. When time allows, I enjoy reading, writing short stories & poetry, playing guitar, working out at Planet Fitness, and practicing at gun ranges. For 15 years I have been a federal employee, working as an officer for the Transportation Security Administration. Functioning as a medic in the Army National Guard for six years, I served a tour of Iraq in 2010. For nearly 13 years I have been happily married to a marvelous woman who teaches high school science. We live near Baton Rouge, LA.

DULCET DYSPEPSIA

A die-hard Lynx never succumbs to pallid music
Unless the antithesis of the song moves sideways
Plastic feelings and flat chords are sadistic
When they wrap you in ennui these days

Leave an iron heart on the railroad tracks
Ah, the euphonic sounds of the sweetest terror
That black heart will derail all and suffer no attacks
Fine champagne will be served with great fervor

Non-Euclidean dancing may resume the tunes
As lines become circles on the G clef
If only this could happen real soon!
Oh, how the world has grown tone deaf!
Genius is gone, only mediocrity is here
Lost is the music of the spheres....

NO MEAL TICKET

A bitter voice calling from the past
Greedy hand outstretched as if winning a lotto fast
Wait a century for each grain of sand
What part of NEVER do you not understand?

I have no mercy for those who refuse to face facts
Pray in vain regardless of your acts
A trillion-watt star does not require a five-watt light
What does it take to get you out of my sight?

No, I am not aroused by your tenacity
I become nauseous and infuriated at such audacity
Suffer alone as you have no worth
From my vantage I laugh with illimitable mirth!

TRUNCATED

I am proud to be of the Alien Elite
Yet my fealty is quite discreet
There are eighteen keys, a trapezoid, and seven towers
But the Black Flame is my true source of power
Seeking no approbation, I do not proselytize
To the dismay of most We cannot be compartmentalized
The Ark and the Grail are decoys in history
Better luck with alchemy or the Anunnaki
Masonry, Bohemian Grove, and Bilderberg Group
All a mess of conspiracy theory soup!
Wicca and the O.T.O. only build a juvenile transcript
You might as well study the Voynich manuscript!

Epiphany lies behind your eyes if you would only check
It is there you will find the "Great Architect"
Faith is a "gift" granted to the lot of fools
Do not "believe", lest you become one of Our mules
If you are wise you will clearly see....
This is a religion of pure practicality!

These pieces were inspired by such Satanic concepts as laughing at the herd, the phenomenon of tapping into music for magical power, the idea that "everyone is a star" but we all shine at different wattage, the collective unconscious, and the fact that Satanism is a practical religion as opposed to a hokey, mystic, or spooky occult one.

WILLIAM TULL

William Tull is an American speculative fiction and horror author. When not writing, he can be found raising goats and exploring the outdoors with his family, making experimental films and music, or venturing into the past via medieval reenactment. His interests include historical research, gaming, and long walks on the black sand beach at the edge of The Void.

LUCIFERI EXCELSI

The shining star of morning,
Withered, hollow earthly light.
Dire sign of trembling warning,
Broken shackles, might makes right.

Brimstone, sulfur, adamantine gate,
Greet me brother! It is the signs of Hell.
Passion, purpose, righteous hate,
Welcomed, joyous, Oh they know me well!
Walk beside me Virgil,
Show me without fear.
Hecate, Loki, Ba'al, Nergal,
Bequeath to me Longinus' spear.

Descend below, the circles nine,
Each one I make my home.
Sinners drink their ashen wine,
Polish my crown of Judas chrome.

JOY BUZZER

Who is the one who put the tack in the chair?
The salt in the sugar?
The gum in the hair?
He never plays fair.

Who is the one with the squirting corsage?
The hot pepper gum?
The mirrored mirage?
An ego massage.

Who is the one with the disappearing ink?
The shocking joy buzzer?
The bombs that stink?
The friend's ship will sink.

Who is the one with the itchiest powder?
The slide whistle note?
The shells in the chowder?
His clown nose honks louder.

Who is the one who can take you down a peg?
Put you in your place.
With another chalk egg.
He's just pulling your leg.

GNASHING OF TEETH

Blasphemy
Heresy
These are the words you chose to define me.

Heathen
Pagan
Raw stones you chose to throw at a dragon.

Outcast
Outsider
Behold, my pale horse, and me atop. The rider.

Judged
Begrudged
I stand above, beyond, alone. Not budged.

Fear
Insecurity
I have embraced the alien in me.

Exiled
Banished
Your hunting hounds waste away famished.

Risen
Returned
From the ashes of the witches you burned.

Unbroken
Unburied
It was not my casket you carried.

Victory
Defeat
Pissing on the God, who lays dead at my feet.

The inspiration for my pieces is plucked from various branches on Anton LaVey's core Satanic Philosophy. As I contemplated each piece I tried to focus on the specific areas and essays I have returned to most frequently over the years. Foremost, Dr. LaVey's love of laughter and comedy, and willingness to not only face but embrace the silly aspects of ourselves and the world around us. This culminated in *Joy Buzzer*, as a reflection on the role of the prankster in our lives, akin to the court jester of old. *Gnashing of Teeth* is like an acidic eulogy, recited from the perspective of the Alien Elite to those who would mourn his passing despite having outcast him in life. It is a declaration, and a recitation meant to empower the self and allow you to bury the part of you that longs to be accepted. Finally, *Luciferi Excelsi* is inspired by the practice of Greater Magic. It is hard to distill the feeling of power and raw magic of Satanic Ritual in one poem. To me, this is a condensation of the core emotions and incantations present in the ritual chamber, distilled down to a core set of verses that is meant to excite and empower the reader, as *The Satanic Rituals* does for me.

RYAN REEVES

Ryan Reeves was born and raised in Oregon and attended college in Oregon and Montana. He has an MA in Physical Anthropology and has traveled the world digging up human remains. After his MA he decided against being a professor, so he went out into the world with his beautiful wife. They have been loving life and enjoying each other's company since. He discovered his talent for writing filthy poems and self-published two books. In 2010 he discovered the Church of Satan. The philosophy fit like a glove, and the rest is history. He's a proud Satanist who considers himself a highly religious individual. He enjoys fish keeping, tincture making, and video gaming as pastimes.

US AND THEM

The herd, they think we are accursed
Because we consider us and ours first
And Redbeard's philosophy of power
Gives the herd an awful glower
But we can see with perfect clarity
The reason that they hate this verity
They stare outside their little bubble
And all they seem to see is trouble
Huddled together they are satisfied
To never be considered stratified
A Satanist molds their life like clay
To them there is no other way
A life well lived, this is our duty
The natural world, a thing of beauty

INTELLECTUAL DECOMPRESSION

Light the candles, ring the bell
We call upon the powers of hell
Take a drink and hit our stride
Earth and Water are our guide
Next we give the invocation
Will is focused on creation
With each request we cannot fail
"Shemhamforash!" Sa-tan we hail
Enochian keys out of us pour
"So it is done," there is no more

WWW.CHURCHOFSATAN.COM

Found the website and felt alive
Inspired a plot, I did contrive
Thought I could do a bang-up job
Bringing Satanism to the mob
Bought a website at my expense
And Satanism I did condense
So any bum with a connection
Could easily digest with no reflection
I wasn't a Satanist, no, not really
Though to everyone I insisted shrilly
In hindsight it seems I was a bad actor
Should have read more on the balance factor

I wrote *Intellectual Decompression* as a celebration of ritual. It's fun and sing-song-y. I wrote *Us and Them* to glorify stratification and the book *Might is Right*. Redbeard's Philosophy of Power always stuck with me, and I even have it on the wall in my ritual chamber. I wrote *www.churchofsatan.com* as a stab at all pretenders, shysters, thieves, and scoundrels who attempt to create and promote their own perverse and watered-down version of Satanism. I chose the balance factor as inspiration because Satanism, and running their own "church" or "movement," is beyond their grasp. They should have carefully considered their limited grasp of Satanism before setting out on a fool's errand.

DELILAH CHARMER

Delilah Charmer has been a poet ever since she was a little girl. Her first poem was published in the National Library of Poetry at a mere 10 years old. The written word has always seemed to come naturally to her in an abstract and mysterious way with the use of symbology and creativity. You can almost feel her Infernal Black Flame as you read her poems. It feels as if they indeed do come alive.... Ms. Charmer was born and raised deep in the heart of Texas, where she resides. She is a mother, sister, daughter, companion, businesswoman, and friend. A lover of life who indulges by enjoying music, books, solitude, nature/ space, and her close network of family and friends.

WRAPPED IN DARKNESS

Calling upon the Guardians of Hell
Gathering my Masses
Let My Will be done
Here on Earth
As it is in the Dark Flames
Only strength and boldness do come
No time for weaklings
Or those who are undone
Destroy all who come against me
With Forces of Lightning
Let my Magic wander the Isles of Darkness
Through the cold Ether
Strings of Black
Shiny in the Dark with Waves of Blue
This Unholy Queen has come to Devour you

I AM MY OWN REDEEMER

I Am God
Of My World
Creator
Of My Dreams
Destroyer
Of any obstacle
Lover
Of Life and Lust
Giver
To those who deserve it
Dreamer
Of Worlds

THE DREAM

I am everywhere
I am everything
All at the same time
In the Daytime
As the gentle wind caresses my skin
In the Nighttime
As you see me fly
Across the sky
I can see you from afar
Through any human's eyes
I can see you up close
In the Twilight
Everything goes
It's not too hard to do what I do
In a Magical Woman's eyes
Anything is possible
All of the time

The Satanic Principles that have inspired my poetry are: Vital Existence, Kindness to those who deserve it, Responsibility to the Responsible, Indulgence and Gratification, Acknowledgement of the Power of Magic, Undefiled Wisdom, Vengeance.

ERIC DAVID

Originally from Albuquerque, NM, Eric spent most of his life training in one Martial Art or another. He's been illustrating since the age of three. He's published several books on ASD (Autism Spectrum Disorder), patterns, and symbolism. He is currently working on a PhD in Information Technology (Information Security/Data Analytics). He has been in management for nearly 20 years. Lastly — and most recent — he is a musician specializing in ambient (drone) music.

THALIA MELPOMEME

Through penitent stare suffer like any and no other.
For weight of memory stare back laden and unfulfilled.
Shout aloud joy to find only hollow echoes reciprocate.
Lest purposeful change be made else strength ebb and weakness
thrive.
Too little may thirst grow.
Too much may craving never satiate.
Happiness best be served upon no dish at all for savor's sake.
Only in the now may futures be delved, for time cares not.
Constant be my focus.
Fervor carry my change.
For the face without lines is proof of life lived unsatisfied.

This work was meant to encompass focus, balancing indulgence with abstinence, aesthetic appreciation, and balancing happiness with sadness—for both are part of living. It was inspired by the Satanic principles/concepts/themes by Magus LaVey and *The Satanic Bible* (balance factor, focus of emotional powers, and enjoyment of the here and now) and by Magus Gilmore and *The Satanic Scriptures* (freedom of choice and personal power). Additional inspiration came from the study of other philosophies/research into Greek Theater (Thalia = Comedy; Melpomene = Tragedy).

**

Ronald J. Murray is a writer of speculative fiction and poetry living in Pittsburgh, Pennsylvania.

His published work includes his two dark poetry collections, *Cries to Kill the Corpse Flower*, which appeared on the 2020 Bram Stoker Awards® Preliminary Ballot and was nominated for an Elgin Award, and *Lost Letters to a Lover's Carcass*, from the JournalStone imprint, Bizarro Pulp Press. His short fiction and poetry has appeared in *Space and Time Magazine*, The Horror Writers Association's *Poetry Showcase Volume VIII*, on The Wicked Library Podcast, in *Bon Appetit: Stories and Recipes for Human Consumption*, and *Lustcraftian Horrors: Erotic Stories Inspired by H.P. Lovecraft*, and more.

He has been an Active Member of the Church of Satan for nearly a decade. He is an Active Member of the Horror Writers. When he's not writing, he can be found spending time with his wife and kids, drinking too much coffee and reading.

Lightning Source UK Ltd.
Milton Keynes UK
UKHW011940090223
416794UK00006B/80

9 781736 474839